# Unequal Britain
A Report on the Cycle of Inequality

500,000 OLD PEOPLE
PENSIONERS
SUPPORT GROUP
UP

# Frank Field
# Unequal Britain

## A Report on the Cycle of Inequality

 Arrow Books

To my brother Peter

Arrow Books Ltd
3 Fitzroy Square, London W1

An Imprint of the
Hutchinson Publishing Group 1973

London Melbourne Sydney Auckland
Wellington Johannesburg Cape Town
and agencies throughout the world

First published by Arrow Books Ltd 1974
Text © Frank Field 1974
Diagrams © Hutchinson Publishing Group 1974

Photographs © as follows: © Chris Steele-Perkins pp 2
11 21 25 32 37 52: © Nick Hedges pp 2 32 48 56:
© Mark Edwards pp 2 16 28 42: © Angela Phillips pp 2
40: © John Walmsley pp 11 18: © Euan Duff pp 13
22 51: © A Pache p 8: © Janine Wiedel p 14: © Chris
Schwartz p 16: © Thomson Newspapers Ltd p 30:
© Fay Godwin p 31: © Patrick Ward p 39: © John
Brookes p 45: © Penny Tweedie p 51: © Bill Leimbach
p 56: © Colin Curwood p 60: © Ron Chapman p 62.



Made and printed in Great Britain by
The Stellar Press Limited, Hatfield, Herts.

ISBN 0 09 909820 2

# Contents

# Acknowledgements

This report owes much to the following individuals. Sarah Murray typed a number of the chapters in draft and Jane Jessel prepared the final manuscript for the press and compiled the bibliography. Picture research was by Christine Vincent, Malcolm Wicks commented on the housing section, Stephen Winyard the income and work sections and Francis Bennett at Hutchinson improved the report's presentation.

Frank Field
Chiswick
May, 1974

# Introduction

**Has Britain become more equal since the War?**

Most people would answer 'yes'. They believe that the Welfare State has had a dramatic effect in making people more equal. But has it?

For too long this question has gone unanswered. Since the War there have been many reports which have looked at aspects of the issue, but they take a fragmented view of our lives. The pieces of this puzzle have not been put together before so that we have a clear overall picture of what is actually happening in our society.

*Unequal Britain* brings together the findings of all the major research reports published since 1945. It examines whether the Welfare State has made Britain more equal or, despite previous reforms, whether there is a cycle of inequality into which the vast majority of us are placed at birth.

For the purposes of this report we have divided the population into the standard classes or socio-economic groups. These are:

| Social Class | Description |
| --- | --- |
| I | Higher professional occupations |
| II | Other professional and technical occupations |
| IIIa | Other non-manual occupations |
| IIIb | Skilled manual occupations |
| IV | Semi-skilled manual occupations |
| V | Unskilled manual occupations |

We are particularly concerned with what has happened to social classes IV and V — semi-skilled and unskilled manual workers and their families. The report looks at the differences in life chances and styles between these two groups and those at the top of the social scale, social classes I and II and their families. Sometimes we refer to their formal social status; at other times we use the shorthand of 'rich' and 'poor'.

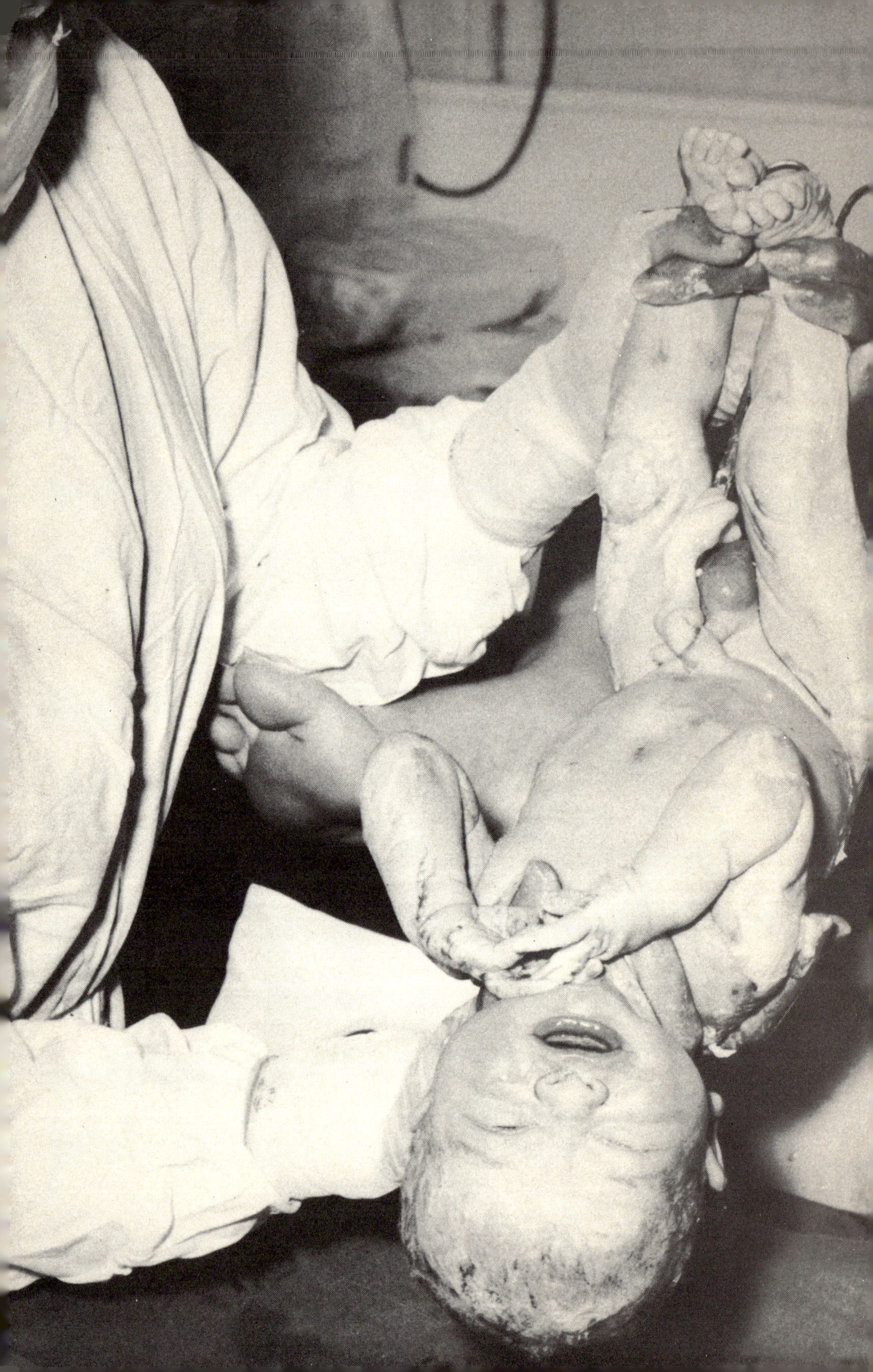

# 1. Birth

**Do children, irrespective of their family background, have an equal chance of surviving birth?**

To answer this question we need to look at the infant mortality rate (death during the first year) according to the social class of the baby's father, and then to see how the situation changes over the years.

## Infant Mortality 1911-1950

Some years ago J. N. Morris and J. A. Heady analysed the 80 000 still-births and infant deaths in England and Wales during 1949–1950, comparing them with data for 1911. They wanted to see whether the inequalities between different occupational and class groups had narrowed during the 40-year period under study.

Their findings showed that although there had been a dramatic reduction in infant mortality, the occupational and class differences remained stubbornly the same. They wrote: 'Following the post-neonatal rate for the individual occupational groups it can be seen that . . . there is a continuous decline in each group from 1911 to 1950.' But they went on to say that: 'the fall for each occupational group is about *the same proportion*.'

In 1911, for example, the post-neonatal mortality rate (death during the first four weeks) of the children of miners was four times as high as of children of professional workers. In 1949-50 the rate for miners' children was still about four times as high as the rate for children of professional men and more than four times higher than the lowest rate in the period. Morris' and Heady's conclusion was that: 'The gap between the highest and the lowest rates was thus, if anything, somewhat greater in 1949-50 than in 1911.'

The authors also analysed the data according to social class. They found that: 'The rough equality of decline demonstrated for the occupational groups occurs also when the occupations are grouped together into the conventional five "social classes".' And they added: 'There has been no narrowing of the social gap in infant mortality; if anything it may have widened slightly. This finding was unexpected.' (Morris and Heady, 1955, 345-8).

The authors proposed a number of reasons why the poor had not improved their relative position. The most important was that the Welfare State reforms of the 1945 Attlee Government would take time to have effect on the cycle of inequality. Has this belief been borne out by the facts?

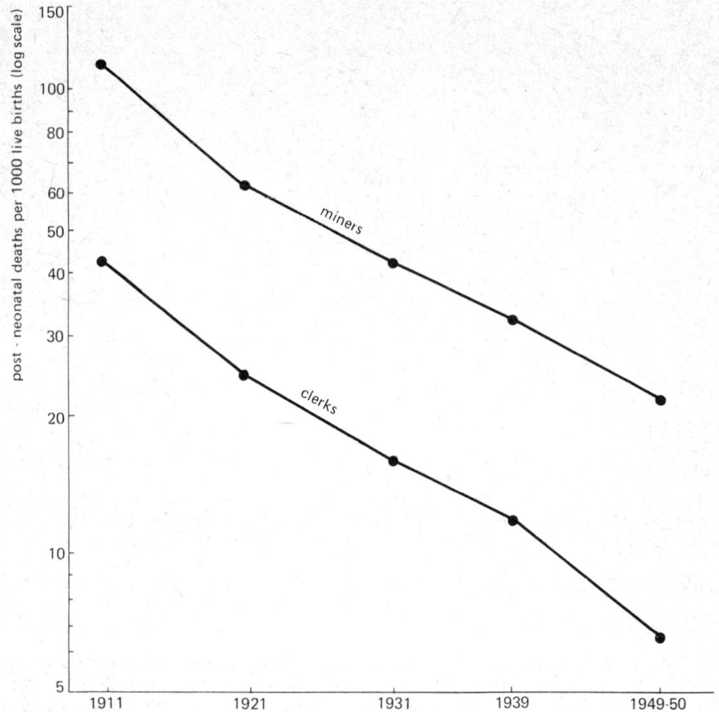


There have been three major post-war studies of this question.

## 1 Infant Mortality 1946

J. W. B. Douglas looked at all confinements in Great Britain during the first week of March 1946. This is the first of two cohort, or on-going, studies we shall be drawing upon in this report.

He made a comprehensive analysis of the life-styles and chances of this group of children by examining the varying mortality rates of babies according to their social class. He noted that there were considerable social class differences in death during the first month of life, and showed that approximately half the deaths were of premature infants (children who weighed 5½ lb. or less at birth).

Dr Douglas then went on to consider which mothers were most likely to give birth to a premature baby. He concluded that : 'Prematurity was least common in the most prosperous groups ; 4.2% of the children of professional and salaried workers were premature as compared with 6.5% of those black-coated workers, 6.7% of manual workers and 7.2% of agricultural workers.' (Douglas, 1958, 66)

Prematurity, therefore, partly explained the social class differences
in the infant mortality rate. Amongst children whose fathers were
classified as manual workers it was very nearly twice that of children
whose fathers were professional or salaried workers.

### 2 Infant Mortality 1958

The second major perinatal mortality survey was carried out in 1958.
Information was gathered on practically every baby born in England,
Wales and Scotland in the week 3–9 March ; in all, 17 000 children.
The results were similar to Dr Douglas's in the differences in infant
mortality rates according to social class. Amongst the 17 000 children
it was found : 'There is a rise from a mortality ratio of 69 in social class
I to 128 in social class V. With unmarried mothers the mortality for
the foetus was even higher at 140 per thousand births.' (Butler
and Bonham, 1963, 20)

The conclusion we can draw from these cohort studies is similar
to that of Morris' and Heady's report of 1911–1950. The differences
in the mortality ratio for children born to the richest and poorest
parents do not show any significant changes during the ten years
which elapsed between the two studies.

### 3 Infant Mortality 1964

The latest detailed study of the infant mortality rate is the 12-month
period from 1 April 1964 to 31 March 1965. The authors, Spicer and
Lipworth, looked at the number of still-births, the neonatal rate and
the postnatal rate (death after the fifth week but before the first
birthday).

Analysing the still-births during the year of study, they wrote :
'It appears that children born to mothers of social class III have a
higher mortality than those of classes I and II. The mothers of social
classes IV and V combined were worse off still, but the greatest
change was between mothers of social class III and those of higher
social classes.' (Spicer and Lipworth, 1966, 8)

Commenting on the changes in infant mortality since the previous
study in 1949-50, the authors reported : Social classes I and II
combined, which had lower still-birth rates than other social classes
in both investigations, fell by 41% in 1964 as against only a 23%
reduction in social classes IV and V.' (Spicer and Lipworth, 1966,
3–4)

The changes in the neonatal death rate were described in the
following terms : 'Again the percentage reduction in rates of social
classes I and II was greater than that for the lower social groups but
the difference was less marked.' (Spicer and Lipworth, 1966, 4)

On post neonatal deaths the authors reported : 'Social classes IV
and V show the greatest reduction in post neonatal rates, but this
may have been due to an exceptionally low respiratory death rate in
the study year.' (Spicer and Lipworth, 1966, 4)

The damaging conclusion of these reports is that there has been no dramatic narrowing of class differences between the survival of rich and poor children. As one expert has written : 'Recent information on infant mortality shows that the gap between classes is actually widening over time. In England and Wales in 1964–5 the incidence of infant death was more than half as high again in social classes IV and V as in classes I and II.' (Gough, 1970, 213)

This is the first link in the cycle of inequality.

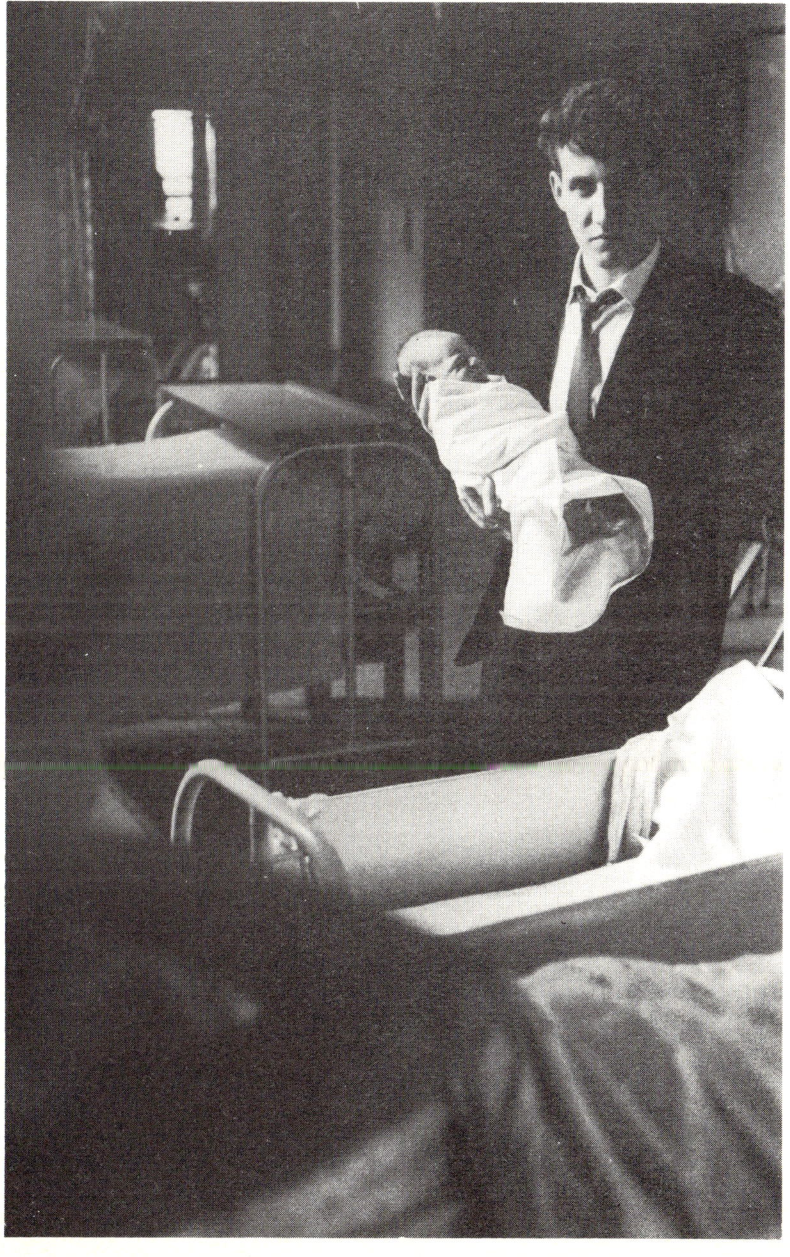

WHEN 50 PEOPLE COME, WE TAKE £
WHEN 35 PEOPLE COME, WE TAKE £5
MONEY SPENT
RAFFLE PRIZE = £1
25
5
TOTAL

# 2. Education

**How fair is our education system ? Does everybody have an equal chance of getting on ?**

Ever since the *Early Leaving* report we have become aware of how important a parent's class is to the type of education a child receives. In this section we shall be drawing on the major education reports published during the last twenty years, and we shall take as our starting base the *General Household Survey* (*GHS*). Its usefulness lies in its ability to look at society as a whole and establish the relevance of social background to all forms of education, and of education to employment, earnings and so on.

## Equal at the Start ?

We all know that children come from vastly different home backgrounds and that this affects the child's life chances. Indeed, 'there is a sense in which the educational system itself contains a built-in bias in favour of middle-class children . . . in that children from middle-class homes find in the school situation basically the same values as they experience at home.' This view comes from Ronald Davie and his colleagues who followed up progress made by the children in the second cohort study in 1958 – known as the National Child Development Study. They wrote :

By the time children start school, they have acquired an orientation to the world embracing norms and attitudes which affect their response to school. Many working-class children will find these norms and attitudes are in significant respects different from those adopted by the school ; they will tend to be judged by standards which are alien to their previous experience. (Davie, Butler and Goldstein, 1972, 28)

## Home Background

Can our education system help to redress the inequalities in home life ? One important way to lessen the differences would be for children from poorer homes to start school earlier than other children. The *GHS* shows, however, that in practice the reverse occurs – schooling before the age of five was 'considerably' more common amongst children from homes where the father was following a middle-class occupation. (*GHS,* 232)

## Primary Schools

What happens to children once they are at school ? Are the inequalities in their home backgrounds overcome, or do children become more unequal ?

Reporting on the 1946 cohort study, Douglas stated that during the years of primary schooling the gap in attainment between children from different occupational groups begins to widen. (Douglas, 1964) In a later study he suggests that this trend continues into secondary schooling. (Douglas, 1968)

This finding rightly brought into debate the 11 + examination and the tripartite education system (divided into grammar, technical and secondary modern schools) which results from it. But:

the laudable attempts to provide equal opportunity for all children have perhaps overlooked the very marked inequality which exists even before children transfer to junior school. This is partly because very few studies have been concerned with attainments in infant schools or departments, and even fewer have related these attainments to social class. (Davie, *et al.*, 1972, 98-9) The National Child Development Study therefore went on to undertake such an analysis.

It found a strong association between social class, reading and arithmetic attainment at seven years of age.

The chances of an unskilled manual worker's child (social class V) being a poor reader are six times greater than those of a professional worker's child (social class I). If the criteria of poor reading are made more stringent, the disparity is much larger. Thus the chances of a social class V child being a non-reader are fifteen times greater than those of a social class I child. (Davie, *et al.*, 1972, 102)

Overall the differences between children of different backgrounds are to be clearly seen by the age of seven. According to the report: 'The estimated gap in terms of average reading performance of the most and the least advantaged child . . . was over four years.' (Davie *et al.*, 1972, 190) So we find that the inequality existing before children reach school is *increased* by their early schooling.


## Secondary Schools

Does secondary education reduce or reinforce these inequalities? For a long time the evidence has shown that children from poorer homes are not fully represented in what are commonly regarded as the better secondary schools. The first study to show this, published in the mid-fifties, reported that the sons of clerks had four or more times as good a chance as the sons of unskilled manual workers of attending a grammar school. (Floud, Halsey and Martin, 1956, 42)

The position has not changed since then. The *GHS* found that secondary modern schools still contain a higher than average proportion of children from blue-collar groups; whereas grammar, direct grant and independent schools contain higher than average proportions of children from professional homes. Thirty-eight per cent of all schoolchildren came from the homes of white-collar workers. But these children accounted for 59% of all grammar school pupils and 84% of 11–14-year olds in direct grant and independent schools. (*GHS*, 233)

PARENTS ARE NOT ALLOWED INTO THE PLAYGROUNDS
BEFORE SCHOOL, DURING SCHOOL HOURS, AT DINNER
TIME, OR AFTER.
IF YOU WISH TO SEE THE HEAD TEACHERS & HAVE NOT MADE
AN APPOINTMENT, YOU MUST ASK THE SCHOOL-KEEPER
TO MAKE AN APPOINTMENT FOR YOU, OR IF YOUR BUSINESS
IS URGENT, ASK TO BE SHOWN TO THE HEAD TEACHERS
OFFICE. IF THE SCHOOL-KEEPER IS NOT ABOUT, ASK TO
SEE THE SECRETARY.

This means that the inequalities between children *grow* while they are at school. The gaps continue to widen when we look at who spends most time at school.

## Who Leaves First ?

The *Early Leaving* report was the first study to express concern that children from poorer homes were more likely to leave school as soon as they could. While 7% of boys from professional homes left school prematurely, over 38% of boys from poor homes left as soon as they reached the minimum school leaving age. The report noted that early leaving was even more marked amongst girls from a poor background. (*Early Leaving,* 1954, 38)

*Social Class of early leavers. (Source:* Early Leaving*; 1954)*

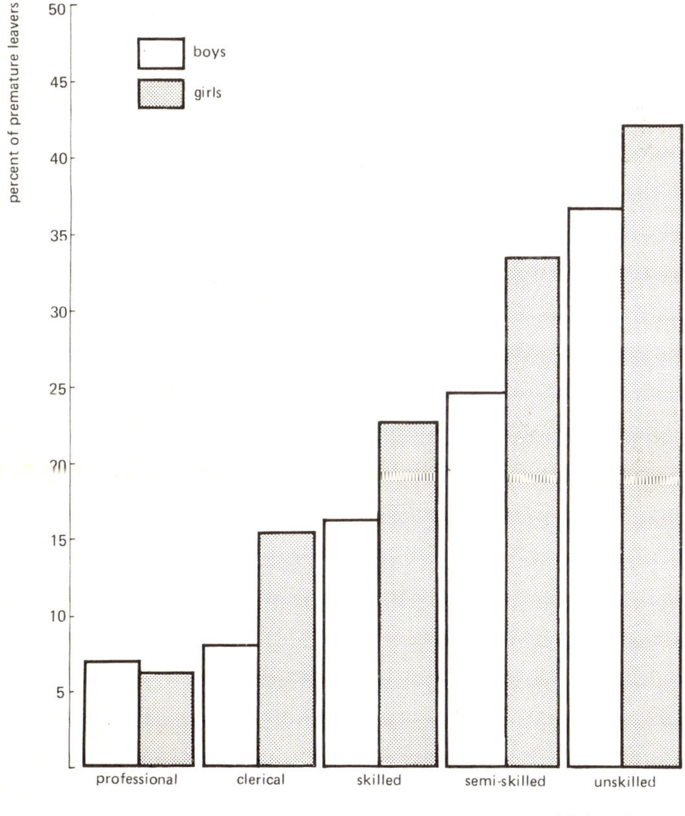


Has this wastage of ability from poorer families changed significantly during the last few years ?

The *GHS* was carried out when the minimum school-leaving age
was 15. The *Survey* found that:

The over-15s made up 13% of all those in full-time education
in England and Wales.
And yet 50% of those living in their fathers' households and
64% of those living away from home and in full-time
education came from non-manual backgrounds.

The *Survey* concluded that there was: 'a considerable over-
representation of full-time students aged fifteen-plus amongst the
professional and managerial groups and a similar under-representation
amongst the semi-skilled and unskilled.' (*GHS*, 233)
Why is this? Are children from poorer homes less intelligent than
other children? The answer is certainly 'no'. The Robbins report
wrote: 'The proportion of children with measured intelligence
between 115 and 129 who entered full-time higher education is
34% for middle-class children and only 15% for those from manual
working-class homes.' (Robbins report, 1963, Appendix 1)
In other words the chances of children of equal intelligence
staying on to higher education is significantly affected by other
factors, such as their home background, and not their measured
intelligence.


## Further Education

When we look at the numbers of students in further and higher
education we find that they are drawn fairly evenly from manual
and non-manual backgrounds. But because manual workers'
children are more numerous than the children of other groups, this
means that it is still more likely for someone from a non-manual
background to become a student than for a child from a manual
background. Further, this group includes students undertaking
part-time as well as full-time courses. Students in higher education,
who undertake full-time courses, are much more favoured than
those undertaking part-time courses in further education, and yet
to quote the *GHS* again: 'Part-time students at colleges of further
education come predominantly from skilled manual workers'
homes.' (*GHS*, 236)
The kind of institution one attends after the age of fifteen affects
the level of qualification one is likely to receive – a qualification
which is important in determining the rewards obtained from work.
This is the next link in the cycle of inequality.


## Education and Earnings

What is the impact of education on the amount earned from full-time
work? The *GHS* spells out that the longer one spends in education
the greater will one's rewards be from work. Of males aged fifteen
or over who attended a secondary modern school, over 59% were

found to be earning less than £1 500 while only 0.8% were in the
£3 000 + a year class. This contrasts with 11.1% of degree holders
earning less than £1 500 while 33.3% earned in excess of £3 000.
These inequalities, of course, would be even more marked if we
took age differences into account. The *GHS* concluded that : 'Those
who had a college education, and particularly a university education,
succeeded in commanding much better salaries. Two-thirds of the
latter earned over £2 000, almost twice the proportion of any other
group.' (*GHS*, 242)

## Qualifications and Earnings

Linked to the length of our education are the qualifications gained,
and these complete the transition from the inequalities in our
educational system to those in the work place. For example, 44% of
male workers with a degree or equivalent earned £3 000 or more.
Only 1.8% of male earners with GCE or equivalent qualifications
earned this sum. Similar, but more marked, inequalities were found
for the earnings of women.

Far from school breaking into the cycle of inequality we find the
inequalities at birth continue to widen during school years. A second
link in the cycle is established.

SUNDERLAND
EDUCATION AUTHORITY
CAREERS
OFFICE
HOURS OF OPENING
MONDAY
TUESDAY
WEDNESDAY
THURSDAY
FRIDAY
PLEASE NOTE
THIS OFFICE IS CLOSED

# 3.  Income

## Income from Work

### What differentials in income exist between the rich and poor, and have these changed during the post-war years ?

One fact stands out above all others ; we still know very little about the income of the rich. In *Some economic curiosities of the British wage structure* Barbara Wootton commented :

In contemporary industrial society a deep reticence pervades the whole subject ; and it is particularly marked at the upper end of the income scale. According to the prevailing code a man's income is one of his economic private parts : reference to it is subject to a powerful social taboo. (Wootton, 1955, 28)

The situation has improved a little since 1955. We can gain a snapshot of the earnings of the employed population from the *New Earnings Survey* (*NES*) 1973. This shows that of the 11 million men aged twenty-one and over in April 1973 who worked a full week, some 1.1 million earned less than £25, while 1.2 million earned over £60 a week. Likewise, of the 5 million women employees who worked a full week, 0.5 million earned less than £14 whilst at the other end of the earnings scale another 0.5 million earned more than £35. (*NES*, 1973)

Similar inequalities exist between the earnings of manual and non-manual workers. The *NES* data show that the average weekly earnings for a male manual worker were £38.8 in 1973. This compared with £46.7 for male non-manual workers. But these figures do not tell us how many hours each group had to work. Earnings for the normal working week made up only 71.5% of male manual workers' pay compared with 93.8% of male non-manual workers' pay. On average male manual workers worked approximately eight hours a week more than their non-manual counterparts for, on average, £9 a week less.

### *Changes in Distribution ?*

Have these inequalities become more or less pronounced over the years ? To answer this question we turn to data published by the Inland Revenue. Although its use has certain disadvantages (the definition of income is very restricted and excludes a number of sources such as fringe benefits) it is the only up-to-date information in answer to this question. (For fuller criticism see Titmuss, 1962.)

The Inland Revenue's view of the post-war years is : 'The broad
picture of the last twenty years is of a tendency for variations between
incomes to diminish.' (Inland Revenue, 1972, 4) This has been
disputed by Chris Trinder, a young specialist on income distribution.
He has examined the share of income accruing to different groups of
the population in 1949–50 (the first post-war study) and in 1969–70.
His findings show that at both points in time the richest 30% of the
population received a share of the total income over 3½ times that
obtained by the poorest 30%. His comment is : 'Over the post-war
period the top 40% actually improved their position and at the same
time the bottom 30% lost ground.' And he concluded his study :
'Even if . . . there were no deficiencies in the Inland Revenue data,

*Distribution of Income by Different Groups.* (*Source: Trinder, 1974*)

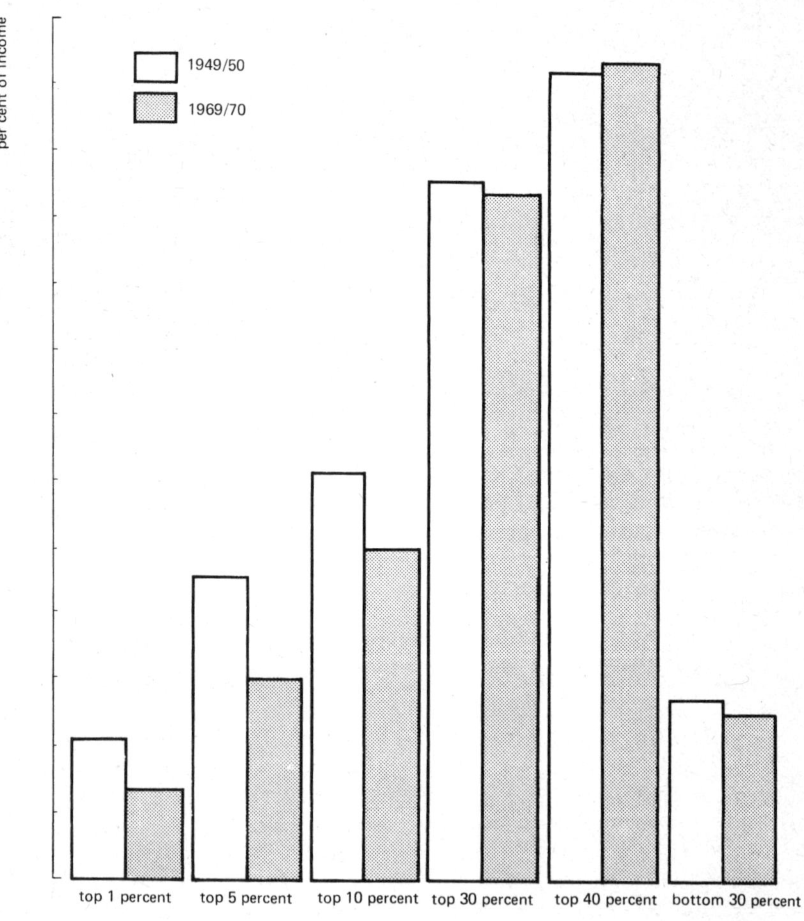

there is still no unambiguous evidence of a clear trend towards greater equality of incomes, and many people on looking at the evidence would claim that inequality had increased.' (Trinder, 1974, 6–7)

This view that the inequality in incomes has not diminished significantly is further supported by evidence from Central Statistical Office (CSO) data. One analysis of this material has shown a reduction in the degree of inequality of income up to about the middle of the 1950s and 'since 1957 equality has ceased.' (R. J. Nicholson, p. 16)

Nicholson's study was of data up to 1963. Atkinson has continued this analysis so as to include data up to and including 1967 – the last year the CSO published estimates on income distribution.

Atkinson's view is that : 'The extension of the period to 1967 does
not affect Nicholson's conclusion that "the most considerable change
is that which took place between 1949 and 1957".' (Atkinson, 1973,
109) Trinder comments on the whole period from 1949 to 1967 in the
following terms : 'Overall . . . it does appear that the redistribution
which did occur was from the top to the near-top income ranges.'
And he adds : 'These figures do not provide much comfort for those
in the lower and middle income ranges.' (Trinder, 1974, 9)

Is Trinder's view that there has been very little redistribution to
those with the lowest income supported by other data ? If it were
true that a substantial redistribution had taken place during the post-
war years, the rewards of the poorest would have improved relative to
other groups. But have they ?

The first official study on wages was made in 1886. It showed
that the lowest male decile's (the poorest 10% of the working
population) earnings were 68.6% of average earnings. The latest
information for 1973 shows the poorest 10% of male manual
workers' earnings as 67.3% of average earnings. So although wages
have risen considerably since 1886, the *share* going to the very
poorest has remained almost unchanged since then.

*Lowest decile of male manual workers as % of average male manual earnings.*
(*Source:* British Labour Statistics, *1971; and* Hansard, *1974*)

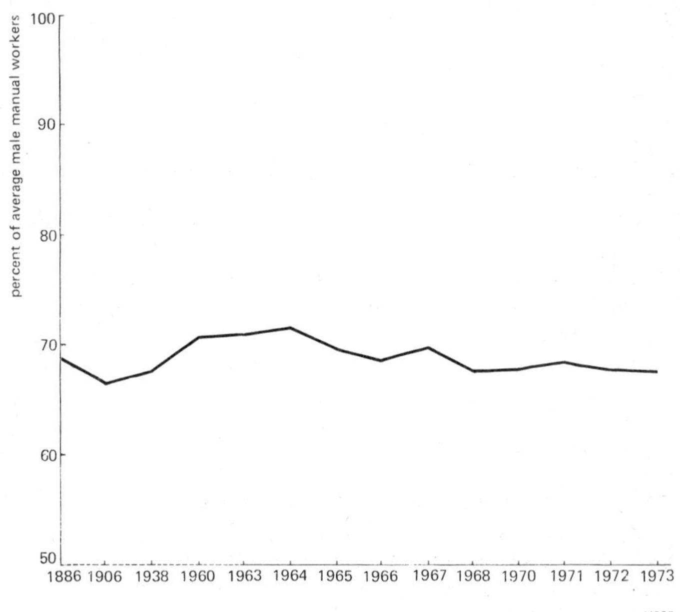


A slightly brighter picture emerges if we study the wages of the
poorest women workers. The first survey of women's wages was
carried out in 1938. The value of the lowest decile of manual female

wages was then 64.3% of the average earnings for manual female workers. By 1968 this had risen to 71.1%, but the latest data for 1973 show a fall to 69.2% (*British Labour Statistics,* 1971, Table 79 ; *Hansard,* 1974). We shall have to wait and see whether the Equal Pay Act, which comes fully into force in 1975, will significantly reverse this trend.

*Lowest decile of women manual workers as % of average women manual workers.* (*Source:* British Labour Statistics, *1971; and* Hansard, *1974*)

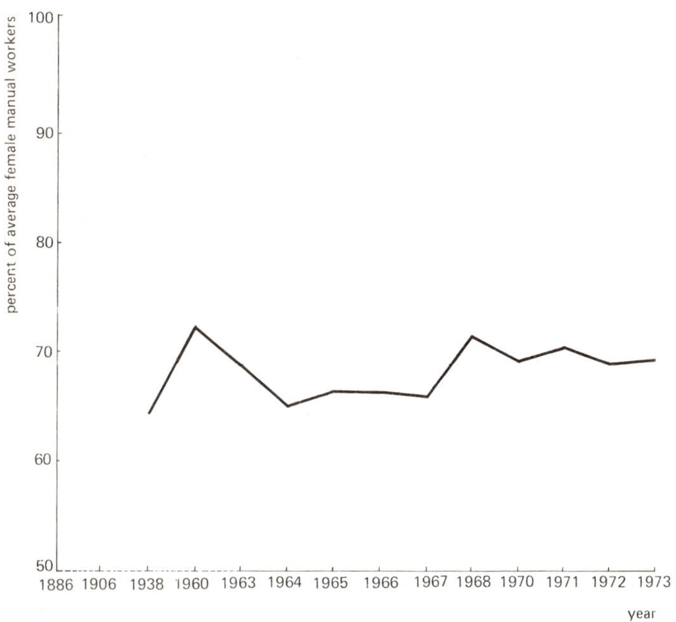


This evidence supports the view that the relative income of the poor has not improved during the post-war years. The gap between rich and poor has not narrowed.

But what has happened to the living standards of the very poorest families ?

### Living Below the Poverty Line

It would be wrong to think that the poorest paid are exclusively juveniles, or wives going out to work for pin money. It is true, however, that many families reach a standard of living just below the State poverty line only because the wife brings home a second wage packet. On the other hand, many families live in poverty even though one or both parents are in full-time work.

The most recent study on the numbers of working families whose income is below the official poverty line was published in *Two Parent Families.* This put the total of working families in poverty at 74 000.

There are also 24 000 wage stop families (for more information see the next section) so very nearly 100 000 families lived on an income *below* the official poverty line, and these families were responsible for the well-being of 300 000 children. (*Two Parent Families*, HMSO, 1971, Table 2)

An analysis made in 1973 by the Department of Employment of the earnings of the very poorest wage earners shows that the income of some low wage earners are subject to wide fluctuations. (See Layton, 1973) And this is even more true of a family's income, particularly when the mother is contributing to the household finances by being employed; when children are ill, or in long summer holidays, many mothers have to stop working. As a consequence the family's income drops. It is therefore important to look at the number of families who are at risk – i.e. whose income is just above the poverty line. So, despite a general improvement in living standards, the *differences* in income between rich and poor have remained roughly the same since the war, giving us one more link in the cycle of inequality.

**Income From Benefit**

**Why do some people become poor when they are unable to work?**

The following section reports on how the higher-paid jobs also carry important fringe benefits — e.g. sick pay and occupational pensions. The poor have to rely often exclusively on State help. But they still remain poor. Why?

It was to tackle poverty caused by the interruption of earnings that Beveridge proposed a major national insurance scheme which would guarantee claimants an income as of right above the poverty line. (The Beveridge Report, 1942) Tragically the Beveridge Report was not fully implemented. Insurance benefits, such as old-age pensions and unemployment pay, were not paid at a value sufficient to raise all claimants' incomes to above the poverty line. Instead, the poor were left with the choice of claiming means-tested assistance or remaining in the most desperate poverty.

The National Assistance Board was established in 1948. In that year just over a million heads of households (including pensioners, sick or disabled married men, and single people) drew a supplement to bring their income from benefit up to the State poverty line.

Thirty-five years later we find a threefold increase in the numbers dependent on supplementary benefit (national assistance was renamed supplementary benefit in 1966). There has been a growth in the importance of other national means-tested benefits, of which there are over forty. The most important of these, apart from supplementary benefits, is the rent rebate and allowance scheme. Over 3.5 million heads of household are too poor to pay the full fair rent on their homes.

*The Poor on Benefit*

At the end of 1972 (latest available information) over 4½ million people's income and well-being were determined by the payment they drew from the Supplementary Benefits Commission. About half of these payments go to people over retirement age. With increasing unemployment and the growth in one-parent families the composition of the poor on benefit has changed during the last thirty or so years. Previously pensioners accounted for three out of every five payments made.

*The Feel of Poverty*

What is life like at or below the poverty line? A family with three children paying rent of £3.50 (a claimant's rent is usually met in full) are deemed to be in poverty if they have an income of £22.45 or less per week. For older children the family would be given a slightly larger benefit.

What do these sums mean in the daily budgets of the poor? Poverty in Britain today means that the State expects parents to provide all

the needs (except rent) of a child under five on a payment of 34p
a day. This rises to 62p a day for a child just below the school
leaving age and £1.20 a day for a single adult. This is the State's
definition of poverty.

*Wage-Stopped Families*

Some people have to exist on less than this sum. We have already
looked at those families where the father earns a poverty wage.
These men, when they are unable to work, are not paid benefit which
is above their normal income, but are wage-stopped. In other words
their benefit is stopped at the level of income they earned when in
full-time work at their normal occupation. At the present time there
are 9597 people affected by the wage stop.

How do families cope with living below the poverty line?

One appropriate source to quote is the Government itself. In a
study of fifty-two families penalized by the wage stop it reported that:

Several families said they had difficulty in finding money for food on Wednesday
and Thursday (i.e. the last two days before the payment of benefit) .... Lack of
variety in food was a factor most frequently commented on, and bread and
potatoes were eaten in large quantities .... The standard of clothing was generally
poor, and keeping the children in shoes was obviously a difficulty with many of the
families .... Similarly, stocks of bedclothes were low and in a few of the families

were almost non-existent . . . . Seventeen of the families said that they had had their gas or electricity cut off at some time in the past and about a quarter said they commonly ran short of fuel during the winter. (*The Administration of the Wage Stop,* 1967, 5)

In a more recent study on eighteen wage-stop families, Ruth Lister has reported on a deterioration in the living standards of Britain's poorest families :

For all of them life was a constant struggle in which every piece of expenditure had to be weighed up against another : a loaf of bread against a bus fare to school ; warm clothes for the children against the rent ; the rent against the bills piling up. They were caught up in a hopeless cycle, living from one payment day to another, the money always running out too soon so that at the end of each week's cycle they were living off bread and marge and were borrowing from neighbours. It is families such as these who have really suffered from the inflation in food prices. A rise in price of a few pence is a marginal irritation to most of the population ; to those on low incomes, fixed incomes, it means having to do without. (Lister, 1972, 4-5)

Because rewards for work are so unequal, large numbers of people become totally dependent on State aid when they are not working. The major benefits — such as unemployment pay and old-age pensions — are not generous enough to guarantee an income above the poverty line. Hence the growth in means-tested assistance for the poor. This gives us one more link in the cycle of inequality.

THINK SAFETY
TALK SAFETY
WORK SAFELY

# 4. Work

**Are the inequalities in income reflected in the work place ?**

As well as answering this question the information in this section is also important in helping to explain why the social life of different classes varies so much. A man who has to work long hours, or is required to work shifts, cannot possibly have the same freedom in organizing his social life as a man who obtains high rewards for working regular hours and has long holidays.

**Hours of Work**

We have already looked at the differences in the hours worked by manual and non-manual workers. We can now take this analysis a stage further. Dorothy Wedderburn reported in 1970 on a survey of work-place inequality. Her findings on the hours of work ran contrary to the popular image. It is widely believed that higher executives are expected to work longer hours than their subordinates. Wedderburn found, however, that most operatives and foremen, 'because of their intimate concern with the production process,' work the longest hours and were more likely to be required to work shifts. Over 40% of establishments expected their manual workers to undertake shift work. This compared with only 7% who made the same requirements of non-manual workers (Wedderburn, 1970, 594)

**Segregation**

The production process itself is a major cause of segregation. While the housing of office workers in a different building from the production has something to be said for it, other forms of physical separation do not. In her survey Dorothy Wedderburn found that : 'some form of segregation was also the rule in nearly half of those establishments where there was a canteen.' And the physical separation of manual and non-manual workers was carried over into the sports and recreation facilities of 40% of the companies surveyed.

Employers who unnecessarily segregate their workers from other staff carry over this attitude to disciplinary practices. One national survey found that :

**98% of operatives were required to clock in**

**90% had automatic deductions made from their pay if they were late**

This compared with

**only a third of foremen who were required to clock in,
a fifth of whom were required to book in,**

**but only 30% of foremen who had penalties imposed against
them for lateness.**

The picture was totally different at the other end of the scale :

**only 6% of senior management booked or clocked in,**

**only 4% were penalised for lateness.**

And while 40% of management were warned that continual
lateness would lead to their being sacked, 84% of operatives found
themselves threatened in this way. (Wedderburn, 1970, 594)


## Holidays

The Moonman survey found that the great majority of companies
granted three weeks' paid holiday to hourly and weekly as well as
monthly paid employees, and four weeks' holiday to senior
management. (Moonman, 1973, 14) However, holiday was worth
more to the higher paid than the lower paid, not just because they
normally earned more, but because the payment was worked out on
the basic wage rather than the worker's normal earnings.

Dorothy Wedderburn's survey highlighted the fact that most of the
employers in her survey gave all grades of workers time off for
domestic reasons, for example the sickness of their spouse, or to
attend funerals and so on. But whereas between 80–90% of
non-manual workers were paid for the periods they were off, only
29% of manual employees were so treated.

A more recent survey shows a deterioration in the rights of lower
paid workers. To quote Moonman : 'Requests from monthly paid
employees for special leave are more likely to be treated
sympathetically than requests from hourly and weekly paid employees,
especially for dental and medical visits and meetings with
professional bodies.' (Moonman, 1973, 21)


## Accidents at Work

Accidents are very important aspects of inequality at work. Every
year about a quarter of a million workers are sufficiently severely
injured in accidents at work for them to be absent for three or more
days. If we also include all those who are injured but not badly
enough to cause absence of this length, it is clear that injuries
through work are a major problem. Moreover, about 500 workers
a year are killed in accidents at work.

The unequal impact of these accidents across the social classes
is evident when we look at the processes which are responsible
for these accidents. Practically all the fatal accidents occur in
occupations dominated by manual workers.

## Sick Pay

Tony Atkinson has noted that : 'The relationship between low pay
and ill health may be a general link between low living standards
and sickness or may be a specific correlation between low-paid
jobs and occupational related diseases. Alternatively, the causality
may run in the opposite direction.' (Atkinson, 1973, 111)
   The reason why low-paid workers suffer, on average, greater
ill-health than other groups is outside the scope of this report. But it
is important to note that absence from work through sickness is much
higher for low-paid than for other workers. What provisions exist to
safeguard the living standards of those people who, at any one time,
are unable to work ?

*Sickness absence by social class and age.*
(*Source: Atkinson, 1973*)

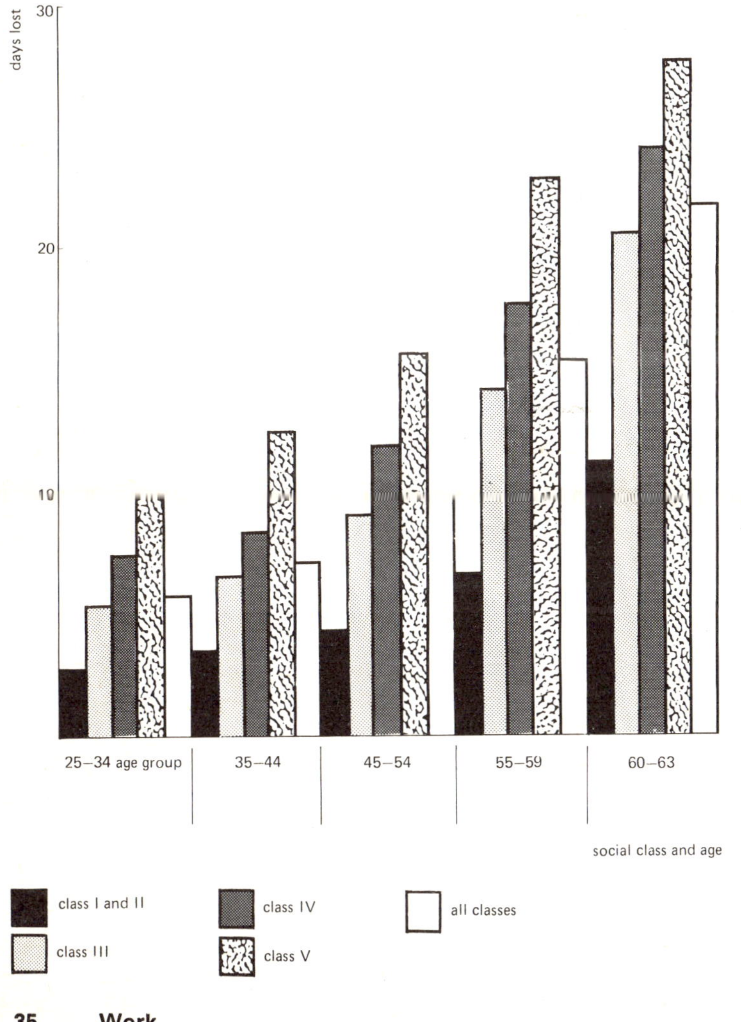

The Government enquiry into the incidence of incapacity for work showed that the absence from work because of sickness was considerably higher for unskilled workers than for all other groups and that this difference became even more marked for older age groups. It also appeared that the illness of lower-paid workers was more serious, for the period of time absent from work was two to three times greater than for professional workers.

To what extent do sick-pay schemes soften the fall in income for those unable to work?

The first major study, published in 1954, found that 56.6% of men, 52·5% of married women and 62.3% of single women were covered by some form of sick-pay arrangements. These figures are somewhat distorted because of the high proportion of married women who were excluded from the survey because they were not covered for national insurance sickness benefit.

The report analysed the coverage by social class. It found: 'There was a sharp decline in the percentage of men covered, from 88.1% for professional and intermediate occupations to 57.3% for skilled occupations, 52.2% for partly skilled occupations and 44.1% for unskilled occupations.' (*Report on an Enquiry into the Incidence of Incapacity for Work,* Part 1, 1954, p. XVI) The report went on to say: 'The analysis for women produced much the same pattern.'

More recently Dorothy Wedderburn reported that of the companies surveyed, 43% made no provision to supplement the national insurance sickness benefits for manual workers. This contrasted with only a tiny proportion of non-manual grades who were without some extra provision from their employer during periods of sickness.

But even those manual employees in a sick-pay scheme were less favoured than other employees, because most sick-pay schemes used the basic pay of workers for calculations. And while 91% of non-manual workers' pay is accounted for by their basic pay, this falls to 68% for unskilled workers who rely heavily on overtime and bonuses to bring their pay up to a higher level.

Wedderburn found that the specified length of time for which the different grades were entitled to sick pay did not vary much. 'But additional time was allowed for operatives in only half of the establishments,' and this compared with 85% to 90% for all other grades. (Wedderburn, 1970, 593)

A further inequality was found by Jane Moonman's survey of fringe benefits. She reported that hourly paid employees usually had to be in the company's employ for up to a year before they qualified for sick pay. Commenting on the duration and amount of sick pay received, Moonman writes that there is wide variation, but 'hourly paid workers fare much less well than other grades.' (Moonman, 1973, 30, 32)

**Unemployment**

Not only are the lowest paid disadvantaged at work, but they are more likely than others to lose their jobs through unemployment.

Nicholas Bosanquet detailed the unemployment rates for different
kinds of workers in 1966. The average rate for all workers was then
2.6%. Professional workers and supervisory grades had unemployment
rates of 0.6% and 1.3%, respectively. At the other end of the scale the
unemployment rates for personal service workers and unskilled
manual workers were 4.9% and 6.8%, respectively. (Bosanquet,
1974)

*Unemployment rates (different groups of workers).*
(*Source: Bosanquet, 1974*)

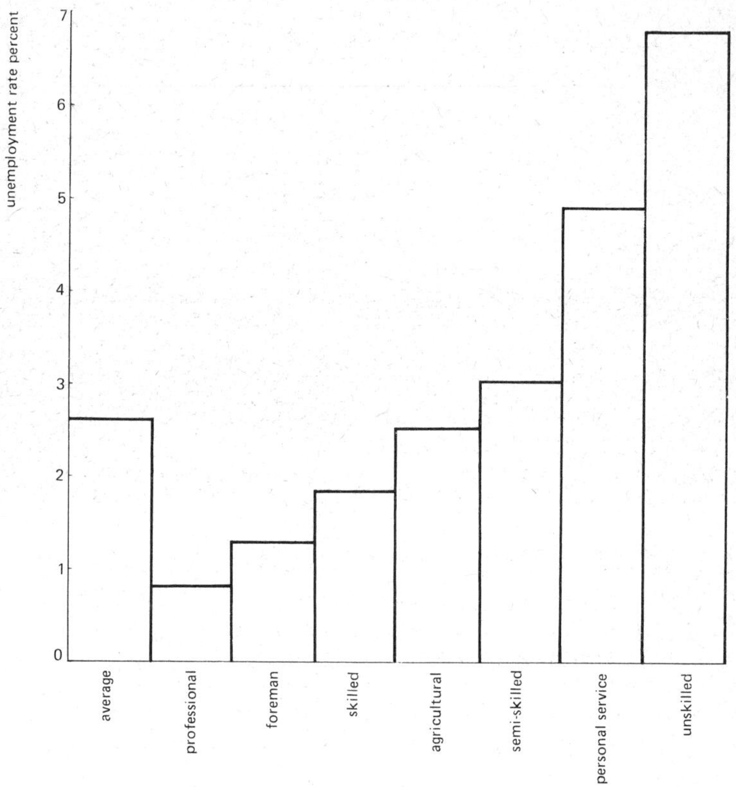


   In the section on income we looked at the provisions for people
unable to work. Unemployment benefits were originally intended to
guarantee claimants an income above the poverty line and, as
additional wage-related supplements are now paid on top of the
flat rate benefit for the first six months of unemployment, this is
usually so. However, 'the low paid worker . . . as a result of repeated
and lengthy unemployment may well have exhausted his entitlement
to the short-term supplement or indeed to the basic National
Insurance benefit. He is much more likely to be among the large
number who depend solely on supplementary benefits.'
(Atkinson, 1973, 110)

## Redundancy Payments

The redundancy payment scheme came into operation in 1967. It covers all employees below the qualifying level for the National Insurance retirement pension providing the worker has given two years' continuous service to the firm. The maximum length of service taken into account for a redundancy payment is twenty years and the workers are awarded payments on a sliding scale towards the maximum amount.

In 1971 the Government published a study on the effects of the new Act. This compared workers covered by the scheme with those outside its scope. One of the report's main findings was that those who draw redundancy payments were not only better off because of the payment made to them under the Act, but they were more likely to obtain a refund of their pension subscriptions, to be treated more generously by the firm's private redundancy payment scheme and to be given the holiday pay due to them. The survey found that if the redundancy payments were taken into account, then the cash available at the time of redundancy averaged out to £380 for workers covered by the scheme but only £30 for those who were not eligible for payments. (Parker, 1971, 84)

OLD AND
COLD
HER
ION
s per week
Issued by H M Government

## Pensions

At regular intervals the Government Actuary publishes a report on occupational pension schemes. The most recent, which appeared in 1971, showed that since 1967 (the date of the second report) the number of workers covered by occupational pensions had fallen from 62% to 58%. But whereas the number of non-manual workers increased from 85% to 87% the number of manual male workers covered by an occupational pension scheme had fallen from 64% to 56%.

A similar pattern emerges if we look at the coverage for female workers. In the four years following 1967 the number of non-manual female workers covered by occupational pension schemes rose from 53% to 56%. Within the same period the number of manual female workers fell from 21% to 18%.

The report also examined the basis on which occupational pensions were calculated. Broadly, there are three such calculations. The first bases a worker's pension on the earnings he drew during the closing years or months of his employment. The second links the pension payments to the salary earned throughout the worker's career. The third paid a flat amount which does not depend on the worker's previous earnings.

The first method of calculation is most favourable to higher paid workers, and 85% of professional workers were covered by this scheme. The least favourable calculation is the third. Not surprisingly 59% of all manual workers who were in a pension scheme were covered by this means of calculation.

The Government Actuary also made an examination of whether schemes augmented retirement pensions once an employee had retired. Augmentation is a means of protecting pensions against inflation. The Government Actuary found that : 'There was little difference between staff and manual schemes' in respect to retirement pensions but he discovered that augmentation was much more common for staff sickness schemes than those for manual workers. (Government Actuary, 1971, 39)

Two private surveys gave rather different results for the number of workers covered by occupational pension schemes. Although Wedderburn concluded that pension schemes showed the smallest differences in treatment within work between different groups of workers ; nevertheless, over one in four establishments had no scheme for manual operatives, whereas non-manual grades were almost completely covered. Moonman found a higher percentage of manual workers covered. 95% of the companies in the survey operated a pension scheme, of these 82.5% of hourly paid and 92.5% of weekly paid employees were within an occupational pension scheme. This contrasted with 100% membership for monthly and senior management employees. (Moonman, 1973, 52)

All the evidence shows that another link in the cycle of inequality is established when we examine the different treatment of people at work.

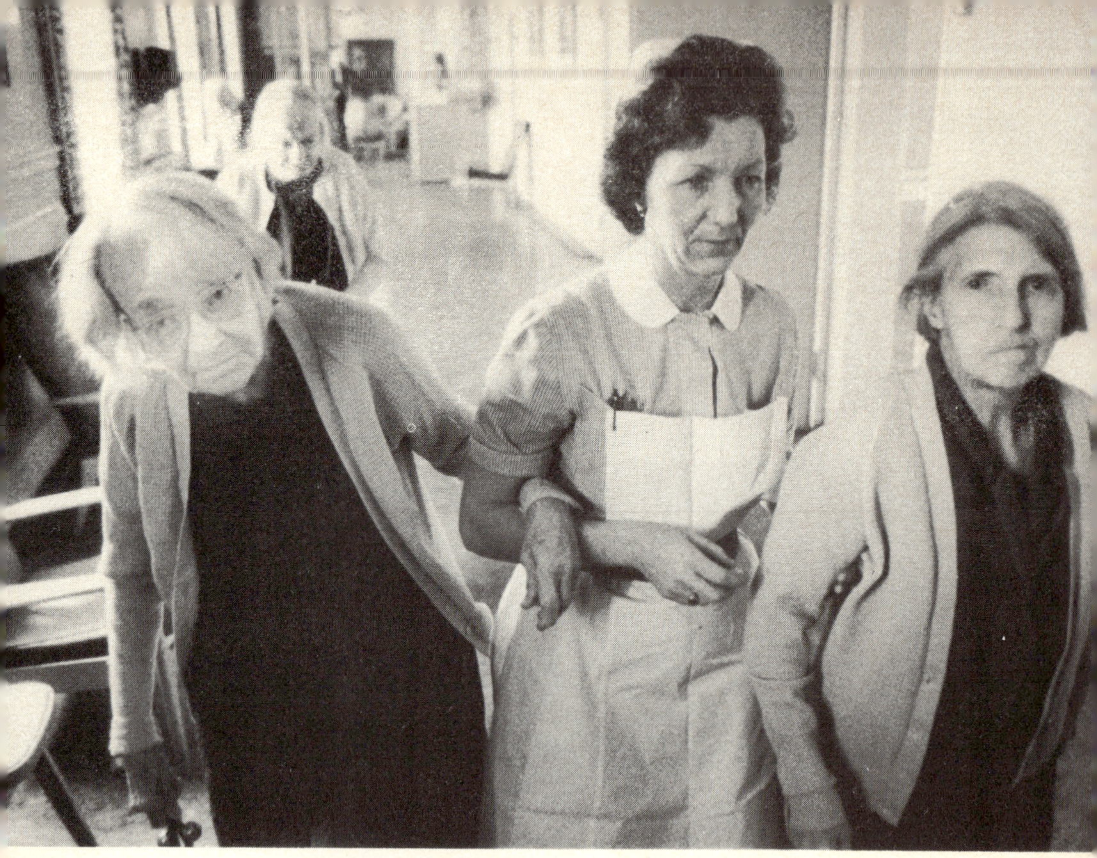

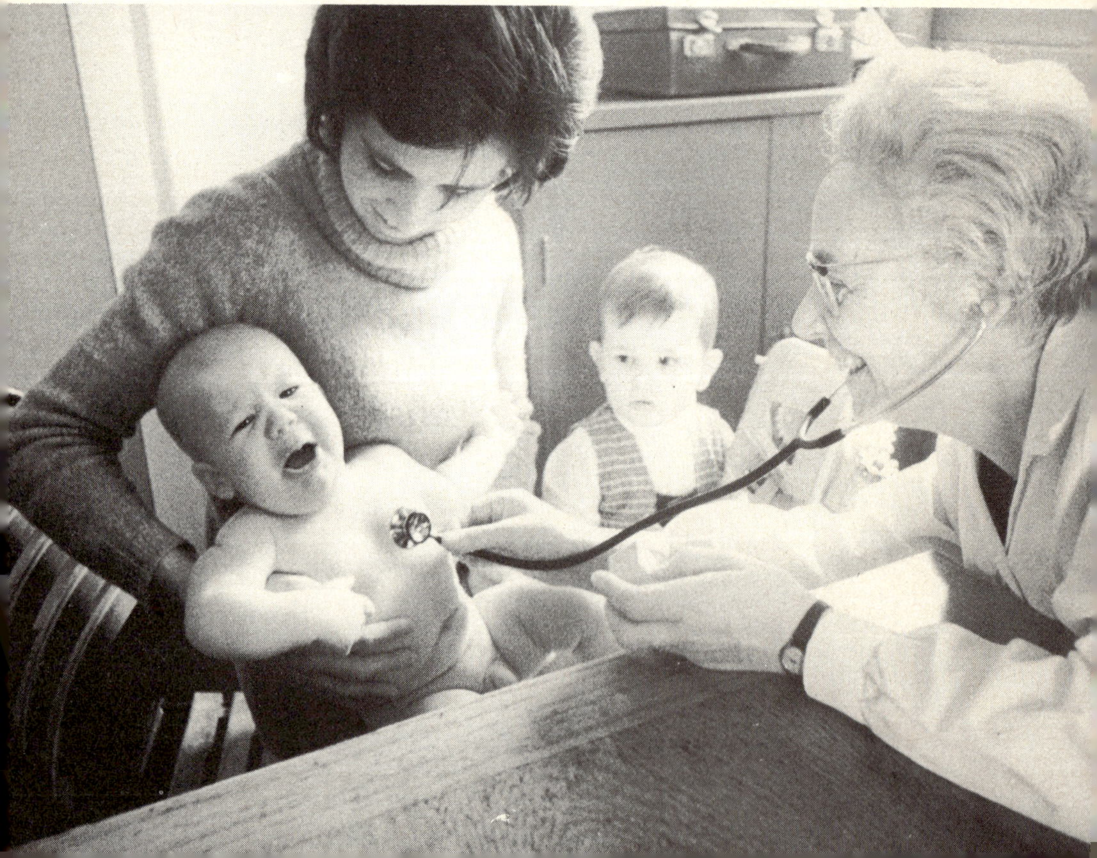

# 5.  Health

**To what extent are Britain's class divisions reflected in differing rates of ill-health ? Are rich people, on the whole, generally in better health than poor people ?**

### Who has the best health ?

During 1961–62 the then Ministry of Pensions and National Insurance carried out an enquiry into the incidence of incapacity to work. The report, published in 1965, looks at the rate of sickness and the days lost through ill-health for each social class.

For the purposes of the enquiry the population was divided into ten-year age bands starting at twenty-five. It also classified the rate of sickness and the days lost through sickness according to social class.

Commenting on this analysis Tony Atkinson has observed that:

The rate of sickness absence was considerably higher for unskilled workers than the average for all workers and this difference was particularly marked at older ages. The length of absence showed a similar pattern, with the number of days being between two and three times as high for unskilled workers as for social classes I and II. (Atkinson, 1973, 111-112)

Over a decade later the *General Household Survey* reported similar findings.

The semi-skilled and unskilled of both sexes have above average rates for each age group. Unskilled men of working age were about three times as likely to say that they suffered from chronic sickness as professional men of the same age group, and younger unskilled men had higher rates than professional men of middle age. (*GHS*, Table 8.10)

### Illness and Social Class

The *GHS* went on to study illnesses by type and social class. It found a clear inverse trend with socio-economic status apparent in bronchitis and injuries, taken as a group. Mental disorders, diseases of the ear and diseases of the digestive system showed a gradient rising from the non-manual to the skilled manual and then to the semi- and unskilled manual groups. 'But even when no trend was apparent, all condition groups except diseases of the eye were more common amongst the semi-skilled and unskilled than amongst other groups.' (*GHS*, 284)

### Use of Health Facilities

Given the greater preponderance of illness amongst poorer groups of the population, do they use the National Health Service more than other groups ? It would be reasonable to expect so, yet experts are divided on this issue.

## Hospitals and Clinics

We have already established the greater birth risks for poorer children – to what extent, then, is this reflected in greater use of health services ? The evidence of inequalities in care in the maternity services is perhaps clearer than that for the family doctor service. Women in the lower social classes at the time of the last survey in the late 1950s were less likely to have had an early examination after becoming pregnant. We have seen in Chapter 1 that mothers in social classes IV and V suffer a greater risk of losing their babies, but one authority has shown that in 1961 these mothers were often not being confined to hospital. (Feldstein, Chapter 8) This confirms the finding that Butler and Bonham came to in their 1958 cohort study. Of mothers most likely to lose their babies 'only 29% are booked for hospital deliveries.' (Butler and Bonham, 1963, 47)

And the follow-up on the surviving children 'leaves no doubt that families in social class V and to a lesser extent social class IV make less use of the many services for children than do other families. It is clear from the results . . . that the children in these groups tend to be the most disadvantaged.' (Davie *et al.*, 1972, 69)

Davie's study therefore confirmed the local studies in Aberdeen and Newcastle which said that, in general, working-class families use health services, such as clinics, food and vitamins, immunization, and so on, less than do professional families.

## Adults and the NHS

What use does the adult population make of the NHS ?

The first study which attempted to see whether the introduction of the National Health Service had brought about a greater equality in treatment was published by Brian Abel-Smith and Richard Titmuss in 1956. After analysing the 1949 statistics relating to hospital discharges, the authors noted that with regard to the admissions to London teaching hospitals social classes I, II and III were well represented, while social classes IV and V were slightly under-represented. However, classes IV and V had a substantially higher death rate between the ages of twenty-five and sixty-four and possibly more sickness.

It might therefore be said on the basis of these data that professional middle-class men of these ages are making full use of the National Health Service hospitals, whereas the semi-skilled and unskilled groups are making fewer demands than might have been expected for their relatively higher mortality experience. (Abel-Smith and Titmuss, 1956, 149)

This view has not gone undisputed. For example, Carstairs has written :

It is apparent . . . that differences between social classes do exist in the use made of in-patient services . . . . Generally there is an upward trend from classes

I to V for most diagnostic groups at most ages. Even where this is lacking, class V is still higher than other classes. (Carstairs *et al.,* 1966, 1000)

But Carstairs, like many other authors, did not consider the last point made by Abel-Smith and Titmuss. Are the poor making fewer demands given their high mortality experience?

## Mental Health

The survey on the incapacity for work shows that inception rates of sickness-absence among working-aged men due to psychoses and psycho-neurosis varied from four per thousand white collar workers to thirteen per thousand unskilled manual workers. Similarly, all the estimates of class distribution on the incidence of schizophrenia have shown a preponderance of schizophrenics in social class V.

We therefore need to consider whether the poor, who are disproportionately found in this group, fare as well in hospital services as other members of the community suffering from physical illness.

One of the few ways, admittedly rather crude, of judging this is to look at the cost of keeping a patient in hospital. In 1968–69 the cost per in-patient per week varied from £49.38 for an acute patient to £16.07 for a patient being treated for mental illness, and £13.49 for a patient being treated for a mental handicap.

While the poor are to be found disproportionately amongst patients being treated for mental illness, the resources spent on patients in mental hospitals is only a third of that spent on patients in acute hospitals.

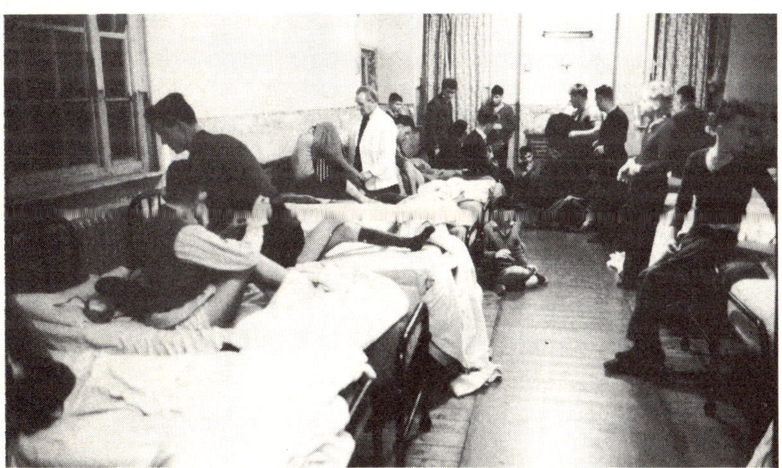

## Family Doctor

Do the poor make greater use of the family doctor service?

In 1964 Ann Cartwright estimated the annual consultation rate for different groups. This varied from 3.5 consultations per year with their family doctor for professional people to six consultations on average a year for unskilled manual workers. (Cartwright, 1967, 31–7) Her findings contrasted with those in Chester where

executives made, on average, the most consultations with their
family doctors.

It is therefore helpful to turn to the *General Household Survey* for
its findings on the use of doctors according to the patient's social
class.

**Overall the Survey found that skilled manual workers and
their families consult their doctor on average slightly more
frequently than do families of professional workers.**

**However, this did not hold for manual workers' children.
Consultancy rates for children under five were almost
twice as great in professional groups as in semi-skilled and
unskilled manual workers' groups.**

**Between the ages of forty-five and sixty-four the position
was reversed with semi-skilled and manual and unskilled
manual workers consulting their doctors more frequently.**

**The position was reversed once again after retirement age
with people who were professional workers consulting
their doctors slightly more than semi-skilled and unskilled
workers, but less frequently than people who were
classified as skilled manual workers when they were in work.**

When reading these results it is important to keep in mind the
greater frequency of ill-health amongst social classes IV and V. No
analysis has yet been attempted to 'weight' the use of the family
doctor service for this factor.


## Use of Dental Services

Bulmer's study, which he carried out in two towns during 1963–64.
showed that the proportion of the population with no natural teeth
rose from 28% and 33% in the two towns among classes I and II
to 56% and 61% among classes IV and V. (The reason for this no
doubt lies partly in differences between the diets of the social
groups, but also the use made of the dental services.) The study of
Chester, which has already been referred to – and which was carried
out in the year after Bulmer's study – showed that the proportion who
had visited a dentist during the previous twelve months rose to
50% for members of social class I and compared with only 16% of
those in social class V. Findings such as these and the differences
made in, for example, preventative medicine led Ian Gough to stress
the need for health education as a pivotal feature of a comprehensive
health service. (Gough, 1970, 218)

It is difficult once again to escape the conclusion that 'Part of the
punishment of being poor is to have on average poorer health and
lower life expectancy.' (Nicholas Bosanquet, 1972)

For all major illnesses there is a greater proportion of poor people
within the ranks of the sick. But surprisingly this does not lead to
their more frequent use of health service facilities.

*Number of teeth present by social class.*
*(Source: Bulmer, 1968)*

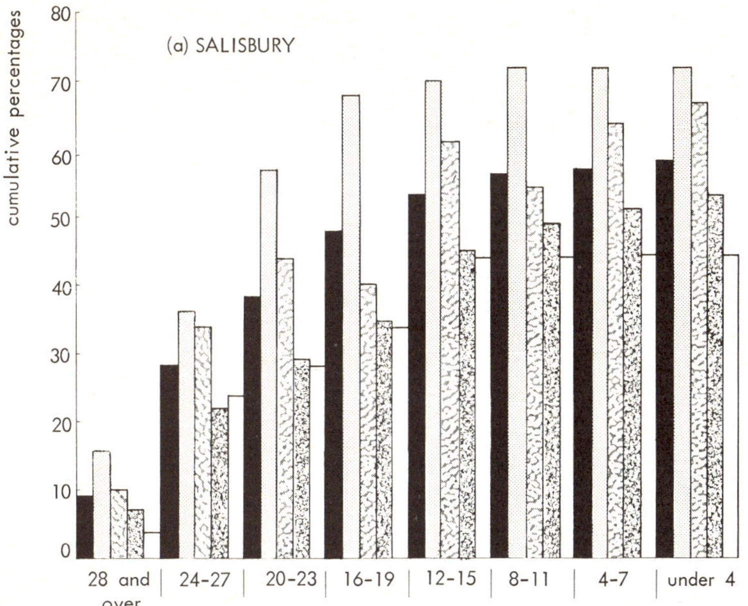



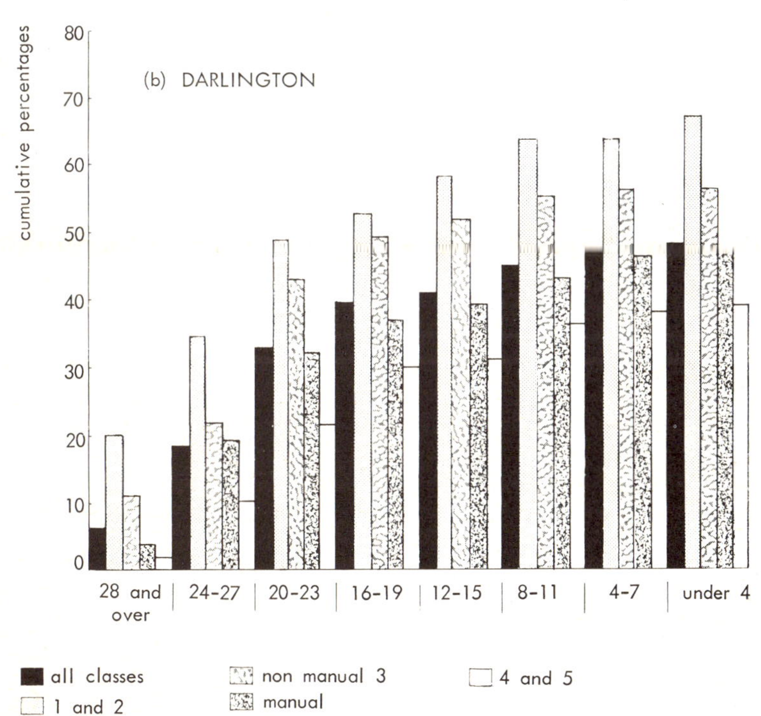



**47      Health**

# 6.  Housing

**Do the poor have equal access to a decent home ? What has been the effect of the growth in council houses on the cycle of inequality ?**

Whilst there is a lot of documentary material by which we can monitor the extent and changes in inequality in Britain, there has only been one national study on the relationship between social class and housing conditions. This was carried out in 1972 and reported in the *General Household Survey.* What follows is based on the *GHS* as well as drawing on other, more limited, studies which help to explain the different circumstances of rich and poor people in the housing market.

To help us understand the present inequalities in housing we need to locate :

**which types of accommodation are most likely to be classified as unfit, or lacking one or more of the basic amenities, on the one hand, as well as which categories of accommodation are most likely to contain the superior housing stock (total number of housing units) on the other hand.**

The second stage of our analysis will examine the chances that both rich and poor have in gaining access to the better housing stock.

The *GHS* showed that in 1971 :

**10.2% of households were owner occupied**

**a further 30.9% were rented from the local authority or new town,  while**

**11.8% of households were to be found in the privately rented unfurnished sector**

**2.7% of households were in the furnished sector**

**5.4% of all households obtained their accommodation either rent free or with their jobs, or from a housing association.**

Which of these sectors had the best and which had the worst housing stock ?

## Unfit Dwellings

The diagram below analyses those dwellings which were classified as unfit for human habitation in September 1971. It refers to England

and Wales and shows that the greatest concentration of unfit
dwellings is in the privately rented sector. (*Social Trends,* 1972, 155)
While only 1.2% of local authority tenants (i.e. council) and 3.9% of
owner-occupiers live in unfit accommodation, as many as 22.9% of
private tenants are so housed. (*Housing and Construction,* 1972
Table 23)

*Unfit Dwellings by type of accommodation.* (*Source:* Social Trends, *1972*)

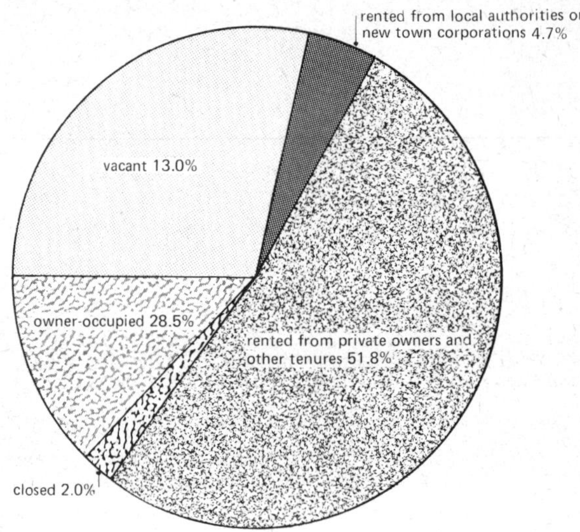


## Basic Amenities

Which types of accommodation do not possess one or more of the
basic amenities ?

The *GHS* refers to Great Britain and not just to England and Wales.
It shows that whereas 90% of owner-occupied houses have sole use
of an inside lavatory — and this percentage rises for households
which rent their homes with their jobs or are in local authority
accommodation — only 51.3% of tenants in the privately unfurnished
sector have sole use of a WC. And this total falls to a fraction over
40% for tenants in furnished accommodation. (*GHS*, Table 5. 13)

A similar position emerges if we look at households with sole use
of a bath or shower. Well over 90% of tenants of local authority
accommodation, or of those whose houses go with their jobs or
businesses, as well as owner-occupiers, have sole use of this
amenity. But only a little over 55% of tenants in the privately rented
sector have sole use of a bath or shower and this falls to 42.6% of
tenants in the privately furnished sector. (*GHS*, Table 5. 13)

Which housing categories are most likely to have more than the
basic amenities and which are most likely to be overcrowded ?

One way of locating the superior housing is to look at the incidence
of central heating. As with all the other issues we are studying in

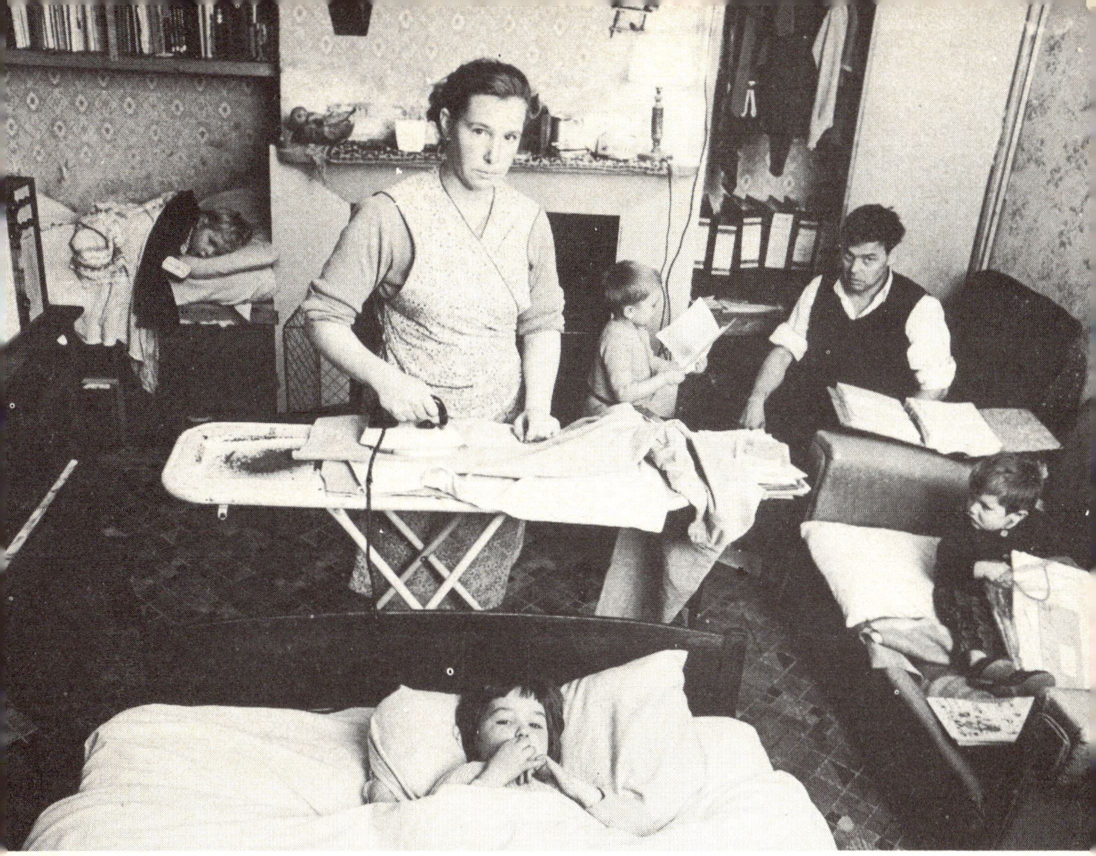

this report, this varies geographically around the country. For example, 54% of all households in the outer metropolitan area of London have central heating, compared with 28% of households in the West Midlands. (*Social Trends*, 1972, Table 106)

But we have to turn to the *GHS* for an analysis according to housing tenure. This shows that a little over 34% of all homes possessed central heating. Owner-occupiers headed the list with a little over 49% having central heating installations. At the other end of the scale only 16.6% of tenants in the privately furnished sector had central heating, and this total fell as low as 8.9% on those tenants occupying privately unfurnished accommodation.

## Over- and Under-occupation

One analysis of the data in the 1966 census has shown that: 'There were 100 000 people in England and Wales living, at one extreme, in just over 30 000 rooms and 100 000 people living, at the other extreme, in 750 000 rooms. (Townsend, 1973, 33) Similarly, another study showed: '9.4% of a national sample of households had one or more bedrooms too few (while) 52.8% had one or two bedrooms in excess of the standard, including 17.1% who had two or more bedrooms in excess.' (Woolf, 1967) But these analyses do

not tell us the incidence of both over- and under-occupation in each tenure group. But the *GHS* does. It shows that:

**3.3% of owner-occupiers had one bedroom below standard**

**7.2% of households in the privately unfurnished sector and**

**17.9% of those in the privately furnished sector were one bedroom below standard.**

At the other extreme:

**44% of owner-occupiers had one bedroom above standard**

**18.6% of households in the privately furnished sector were in a similar position.**

Similar inequalities emerge if one studies households with two or more bedrooms above the standard. (*GHS*, Table 5. 23)

### Where the Poor Live

All the information presented in this section shows that tenants of local authority accommodation, tenants who rent their homes from their employers, and owner-occupiers have, on average, the best housing accommodation. The reverse is true for those tenants who find themselves in the privately unfurnished and furnished sectors. We therefore need to look at the class distribution amongst the different tenure groups.

The *GHS* shows that over 85% of professional workers are owner-occupiers and this proportion falls steadily through the different social groups so that we find that only 21.1% of unskilled manual workers are also owner-occupiers. The reverse is true if we analyse the class composition of tenants in the privately rented unfurnished sector. 2.4% of all tenants are professional workers whereas 17.9% are unskilled manual workers and their families. (*GHS*, Table 5. 18)

Once again we can see that the inequality which exists in other spheres is present in the distribution of housing resources. Unless a poor family is able to gain a local authority tenancy (where the overlap between poverty and bad housing is usually broken) they will have to depend on the inferior private sector.

It is clear that those in privately rented housing often lack the basic amenities and are more likely to be living in slum property. By and large it is the poorest who occupy the worst housing and yet these families are faced with still greater inequalities. Out of their relatively low income many poor families have to pay disproportionately high rents. (*Family Expenditure Survey,* 1963, Table 29) The Francis Committee showed that furnished tenants in Greater London paid on average a third of the head of household's take-home pay in rent. (Francis Report, 1971, 294) And those in furnished accommodation also lack security of tenure. Homelessness is the very extreme point of housing inequality for the poor.

## Homelessness

How do we define homelessness ? The organization Shelter defines a
family as homeless if it lives in conditions so bad that it cannot
lead a civilized family life. The official definition is the number of
people who apply for temporary accommodation. But as one expert
has noted : 'It is important to recognise . . . that the official statistics
(and there are no others) give an extremely unsatisfactory measure
of the problem. *They describe not so much the trend in homelessness
but rather a trend in the provision of temporary accommodation.*'
(Greve, 1971, 59) In other words, homelessness is such a severe
problem that any temporary accommodation offered by local
authorities is soon occupied by homeless families.

When we look at figures on homelessness we are therefore
studying the response by local authorities to the need to shelter
homeless families. Indeed, although the legislation refers to
homeless persons, temporary accommodation is almost exclusively
given to homeless families, and it is only in exceptional circumstances
that other people – single people, childless couples or families with
older children – are given temporary accommodation.

The overwhelming majority of homeless families are expelled
from the private sector. Yet as one writer has said :

Within the Welfare State the bizarre truth is that it is the bad landlord who sweats
his houses and exploits and sometimes terrorizes his tenants, who nonetheless
shelters the new poor. In the absence of the provision of housing as a social service
by the local authority, the paradox is that with all the dislike that the bad landlord
legitimately arouses, he performs a vital social function which exists beneath the
Welfare State. For the poor the choice is often painfully clear, between any sort
of accommodation from a private landlord on almost any terms, and sleeping
rough. (Hilary Rose, 1968, 43-4)

This statement can be supported by evidence from the Milner
Holland Committee (1965) and the Francis Committee on the
workings of the Rent Act (1971).

Has the number of homeless families given temporary accommodation grown in recent years ?

Although the 1948 National Assistance Act gave homeless *persons*
the right to temporary accommodation in certain circumstances,
comprehensive information on the numbers of homeless was not
collected until 1966. But detailed information does exist for Inner
London and this is reproduced in the graph below. It shows a peak in
homelessness in the early fifties which fell away during the next
five years. From the mid-fifties the number of homeless families
seeking temporary accommodation in Inner London has grown.
The latest information, which refers to 1972, shows a total of very
nearly 13 000 people.

Data for the rest of England and Wales are available from 1966.
These show in that year a little over 5 300 people sought temporary
accommodation. This had risen to almost 13 000 people by 1972.
(*Social Trends*, 1973, Table 127)

*Inner London — number of homeless people living in temporary accommodation, 1949-1970. (Source: Greve, 1971)*

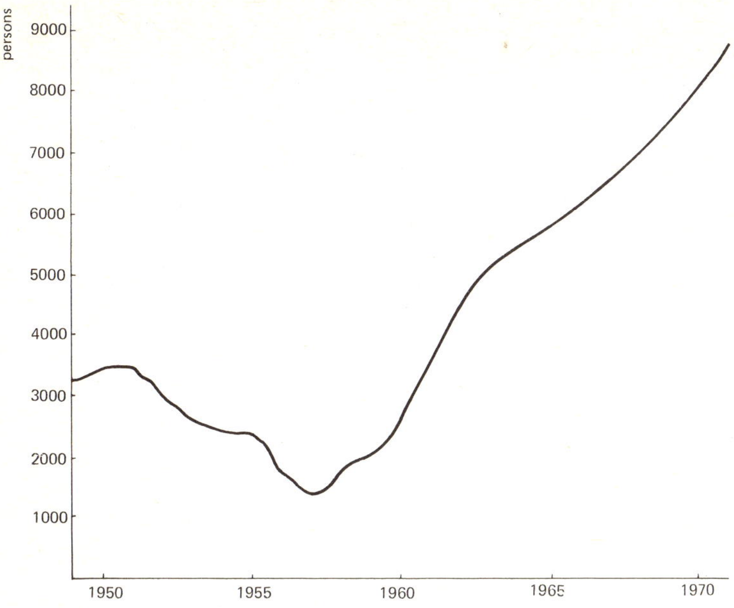

## Causes of Homelessness

Why do people become homeless ?
There are two reasons. First, the privately rented sector is decreasing rapidly and of total housing stock it made up :

**44.6% in 1950**
**26.6% in 1960**
**14.0% in 1971**

And : 'Given the continued demand for rented housing the victims (of this decline) have inevitably been the weak and the poor.' (Wicks, 1973, 3)

The second is also a very simple reason – homelessness is caused by poverty. The first post-war study found that the greatest need for families who had become homeless was for : 'decent housing at a reasonable rent,' and the report went to express that another related need for many people was 'simply higher wages'. (Greve, 1964)

Do these conclusions still hold ? In his report *Homelessness in London* Professor Greve said : 'There is nothing in the current situation to suggest that this is not the case today.' (Greve, 1971, 75)

Some of the very poorest are housed in the worst accommodation and pay high rents. They remain trapped in the cycle of inequality. But we have seen that if the poor are lucky enough to be housed by the local authority they stand a good chance of breaking free of the cycle – but only in respect of housing conditions.

# 7. Wealth

## Is wealth becoming more equally distributed ?

Wealth is an important part of our study for two reasons. First, because it determines the freedom of choice that some people have, and, conversely, the restrictions this imposes on other people who are not wealthy. Wealth is also important because it gives rise to very large incomes for some people. We shall see that, although the ownership of wealth is very unequal, the income derived from wealth is even more unequally distributed.

## How Much Wealth ?

The total national wealth can be divided into three parts — that owned by individuals, that owned by companies and the remainder which is owned by the Government.

The estimate of total wealth in this country for 1966 was £138 000 million. £107 000 million was the value put on total personal net wealth. The net worth of the company sector was estimated at £25 000 million, whereas the net worth of the public sector was put at £6 000 million. In this report we are concerned with the ownership of personal wealth.

*Composition of National Wealth in 1966. (Source: Atkinson, 1972)*

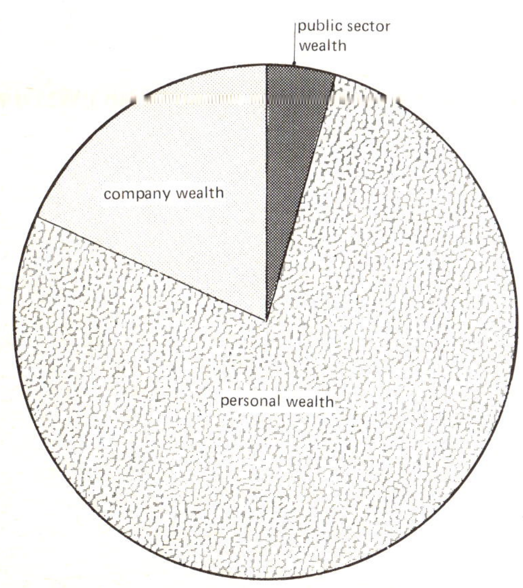

### Who Owns What ?

Tony Atkinson has estimated that 'over a quarter of the total
personal wealth in Britain is in the hands of the richest 1% of the
adult population and that as much as three-quarters belongs to the
top 10%.' (Atkinson, 1972a, 15) On the other hand, over 90% of the
population have wealth holdings of less than £5 000.

Some writers have criticised these figures, notably Alan Day.
He 'guestimates' that in 1973 the top 1% owned 14% while the
top 10% owned 41% of all personal wealth. (Day, 1974) But there
is no question but that most of the wealth in our community is
owned by a very small minority of people indeed. Just how rich
the very rich are can be seen from the money raised from a special
charge put on investment income in the 1968 budget. Ninety-two
people reported an average investment income of £196 000. If
these ninety-two people's investments were giving a yield of 5%
(a very modest yield in present circumstances) each of the ninety-two
had £4 million worth of assets. (Atkinson, 1972a, 16)

### Changes Over Time

It is widely believed that the wealth in our community is becoming
progressively more equal. This is true, although not in the way that
some people maintain. The diagram below shows the changes in the
ownership of wealth of the richest 1% and the richest 10% of the
population in the years immediately before the First World War,
and in 1960. Although there has been a marked reduction in the
wealth held by the richest 1%, from 69% to 42% of the total, the
diagram shows that this has been spread largely amongst the
wealthiest 10% of the population. To quote Atkinson again : 'What
redistribution there has been is not between the rich and the poor,
but between the very rich and the rich.' (Atkinson, 1972a, 10) The
redistribution has very largely taken place within the families of the
rich. The wealth has been spread to children (so as to avoid death
duties) and to wives.

### Distribution of Income from Wealth

Although the distribution of wealth is very unequal, the distribution
of income from the ownership of wealth is even more unequal. While
the richest 1% take 60% of all the income arising from the ownership
of their wealth, the richest 10% account for 99% of the income from
wealth. (Meade, 1964, Table 1)

### Why is Wealth so Unevenly Distributed ?

Three main reasons are put forward to account for the very unequal
distribution of wealth in our society. The first, and rather naïve, view
is that some people are better savers than others. While this is
undoubtedly true, it cannot account for the inequality in wealth. For
example, a man on average earnings saving 5% of his wage packet

*Top income receivers' share of investment income.*
(*Source: Atkinson, 1972*)

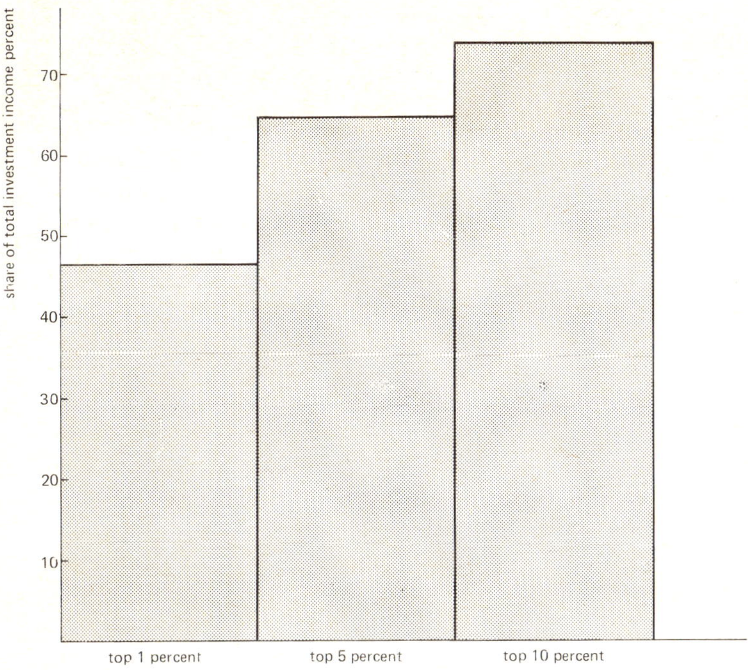

would only save something like £15 000 after forty-five years in work. As one self-made member of the super-rich explained : 'It is obvious, indeed, that mere 'thrift' never made a poor man rich.' (Wedgwood, 1939, 75)

The second reason put forward is that some people are much more talented at making money than others. Again, this is undoubtedly true. Our own society has a remarkable bunch of self-made millionaires. But do they account for most of the super-rich ?

The study done by Professor Harbury shows that they do not. His study looked at the estates of fathers and sons where the son died during 1956–7. He found that two-thirds of the rich sons (with estates over £100 000) had fathers who left over £25 000 (i.e. were in the top 0.25% of wealth holders). This led Professor Harbury to conclude : 'The chance of leaving an estate valued at over £100 000, or over £50 000, was outstandingly enhanced if one's father had been at least moderately well off.' (Harbury, 1962, 867)

Inheritance, then, is the major cause of unequal distribution of wealth. It is very difficult for the super-rich to lose their wealth however stupid they may be. As one American writer has put it : 'The rich by inheritance have a position which they can lose only by a destructive tendency amounting almost to madness.'

A quick glance at the figures suggests that the distribution of wealth is becoming more equal. But the redistribution has largely taken place *within* families and not *between* the rich and the poor. The cycle of inequality has not been broken at this point either.

**59      Wealth**

# 8.   Death

**Does the cycle of inequality carry right through until death ?**

The analysis of the death rate of men by social class was first
carried out from data for 1910–12. These showed that the mortality
ratio rose progressively from social class I to social class V.

One advantage of this approach is that the results take account of
the occupational hazards to which some groups of workers are
particularly exposed. However, if we examine the mortality of
married women according to their husbands' classes, the results
show the class difference in mortality without taking account of the
special occupational risks.

Recent figures supplied by the Institute of Actuaries show
that similar inequalities exist between men of different social
groups. Deaths among male pensioners aged sixty-five to eighty-five
insured under 'work schemes' – schemes for manual workers –
exceeded those of pensioners insured under non-work schemes
by 19% in 1961–63.

The most up-to-date mortality statistics continue to show an
inverse relationship with social class. The occupational mortality
tables give standardized mortality rates for 1959–63 of social class V
which were double those of social class I.

# The Cycle of Inequality

The cycle of inequality is complete. Even in death the significant differences between the rich and the poor stubbornly remain. We have seen that wives of professional groups have a far greater chance of giving birth successfully than the wives of semi-skilled and unskilled workers. The children of professional workers have a far greater chance of surviving the first year of life, and then of living longer.

These children are unequal when they start school and continue to draw away from their peers from poorer homes. The cycle of inequality is reflected in the income earned, the status at the workplace and in the housing rich and poor families occupy. These class differences appear again in the difference in health, and finally in death. As Nicholas Bosanquet comments: 'Class differences in opportunities for life and health start at the cradle and continue through the life span.' (Bosanquet, 1972, 61)

Despite the growth in national wealth the age-old inequalities remain. The position of the poor has improved. But so, too, has that of the rich. It is as if the poor have been placed on an escalator which gradually lifts their position. But the rich, too, are on board their own escalator which is moving just as fast, if not faster.

The existence of the cycle of inequality is well known to the poor, and we are increasingly seeing that they are unwilling to tolerate the injustices which flow from it. In many important aspects we find poor people unwilling to accept the treatment meted out to them, whether in school – with rising truancies – or at work, with large numbers of key jobs going unfilled in the cities.

If civilized life is to continue, the rich must strike a new social contract with the poor to the extent of breaking the cycle of inequality. The report presents the information for a reasonable – yet urgent – debate. The alternative is to break the cycle of inequality on the streets.

# Bibliography


Abel-Smith, B. and R. Titmuss (1956). *The Cost of the National Health Service,* Cambridge University Press.
*Administration of the Wage Stop, The* (1967). HMSO
Atkinson, A. B. (1972a). *Unequal Shares,* Allen Lane.
Atkinson, A. B. (1972b). *Wealth, Income and Inequality,* Allen Lane.
Atkinson, A. B. (1973). 'Low pay and the cycle of poverty', in F. Field (ed) *Low Pay,* Arrow Books.
Beveridge Report (1942). *National Insurance and Allied Services,* HMSO.
Bosanquet, N. D. (1972). 'Inequalities in Health', in P. Townsend and N. D. Bosanquet (eds) *Labour and Inequality,* Fabian Society.
Bosanquet, N. D. (1974). Government and unemployment 1966–70, *British Journal of Industrial Relations,* July.
British Labour Statistics (1971). *Historical Abstract 1886–1968,* Department of Employment.
Bulmer, J. S., G. L. Flack, N. D. Richards and A. J. Willcocks (1968). A survey of the dental health and attitudes towards dentistry in two communities, *British Dental Journal,* **124**(12).
Butler, N. R. and D. G. Bonham (1963). *Perinatal Mortality,* Livingstone
Carstairs, V. (1966). Distribution of hospital patients by social class, *Health Bulletin,* **24**(3).
Cartwright, A. (1967). *Patients and their Doctors,* Routledge and Kegan Paul.
Davie, R., N. Butler and H. Goldstein (1972). *From Birth to Seven* (National Child Development Study), Longmans.
Day, A. (1974) *The Nation's Wealth. Who Owns It?* *Observer,* 20 January.

*Department of Employment Gazettes* (August, October, December 1973; March, 1974).
*Department of Health and Social Security Annual Report* (1973).
Douglas, J. W. B. (1958). *Children Under Five,* Allen and Unwin.
Douglas, J. W. B. (1964). *The Home and the School,* MacGibbon and Kee.
Douglas, J. W. B. (1968). *All Our Futures,* Peter Davis.
*Early Leaving* (1954). A report of the Central Advisory Council for Education, HMSO.
*Family Expenditure Survey,* (1973), HMSO.
Feldstein, M. S. (1971). *Economic Analysis for Health Service Efficiency,* Markham.
Floud, J. E., A. H. Halsey and F. M. Martin (1956). *Social Class and Educational Opportunity,* Heinemann.

*General Household Survey* (1973), HMSO

Gough, I. R. (1970). Poverty and health, *Social and Economic Administration,* **4**(3).

Government Actuary (1972). *Occupational Pension Schemes 1971,* HMSO.

Greve, J. (1964). *London's Homeless,* Bell.

Greve, J. (1971). *Homelessness in London,* Scottish Academic Press.

Hansard (1974). **870,** column 192, March 22.

Harbury, C. D. (1962). Inheritance and the distribution of personal wealth, *Economic Journal,* December.

*Housing and Construction* (1972). HMSO.

Layton, D. (1973). 'Low pay and collective bargaining', in F. Field (ed.), *Low Pay,* Arrow Books.

Lister, R. (1972). *The Administration of the Wage Stop,* Child Poverty Action Group.

Logan, W. P. D. (1954). Social class variations in mortality, *British Journal of Preventative and Social Medicine,*

Meade, J. E. (1964). *Efficiency, Equality and the Ownership of Property,* Allen and Unwin.

Milner Holland Report (1965). *Report of the Committee on Housing in Greater London,* HMSO.

Moonman, J. (1973). *The Effectiveness of Fringe Benefits in Industry,* Gower Press.

Morris, J. N. and J. A. Heady (1955). Social and biological factors in infant mortality, *Lancet,* February 12.

New Earnings Survey (1973), *Department of Employment Gazette.*

Nicholson, R. J. (1967). The distribution of personal income, *Lloyds Bank Review,* No. 83.

Parker, S.R. (1971). *Effects of the Redundancy Payment Act,* HMSO

*Report on an Enquiry into the Incidence of Incapacity for Work* (1964), Part I, Part II (1965), HMSO.

Robbins Report (1963). *Higher Education,* HMSO.

Rose, H. (1968). *The Housing Problem,* Heinemann.

*Social Trends* (1972, 1973). **3** and **4,** HMSO.

Spicer, C. C. and L. Lipworth (1966). *Regional and Social Factors in Infant Mortality,* HMSO.

Titmuss, R. M. (1962). *Income Distribution and Social Change,* Allen and Unwin.

Townsend, P. (1973). Everyone his own home, *British Architects Journal,* January.

Trinder, C. (1974). 'The personal distribution of income and wealth', (mimeograph), Department of Economics, University of Essex.

*Two Parent Families* (1971). HMSO.

Wedderburn, D. (1970). Workplace inequality, *New Society,* April 9.

Wedgwood, J. (1939). *The Economics of Inheritance,* Penguin.

Wicks, M. (1973). *Rented Housing and Social Ownership,* Fabian Society.

Woolf, M. (1967). *Government Social Survey 1964,* HMSO.

Wootton, B. (1955). *Social Foundations of Wages Policy,* Allen and Unwin.